LET'S PLAY

In the Beginning

Words and pictures by Leon Baxter

A LION BOOK

Here is the story of the beginning of the world.

First God made the heavens and the earth. He said, "Let there be light."

God made the sky.
He made the land and sea.
He filled the land with plants.

God made the sun,
the moon and stars.

God said, "Let the sea be filled with living things. And let birds fly in the sky."

God said, "Let there be all kinds of animals."

Finally God made a man and a woman to enjoy it all.

God was very happy with
what he had made.
Then God had a rest.

Help your child get more from this book

As well as reading this book aloud, why not encourage your child to try acting out the story?

Help your child think about their "part". How might it have felt to be one of the characters? What facial expression would they have had? What body language might they use? What might they have said? Use the child's understanding of a human character as a starting point to talk about the place of God in the story.

The picture at the start of this book shows some of the basic "props" needed to act out this story. Their use can be seen in each of the changing scenes of the book. These are only suggestions. If the right materials are not available most children will be happy to improvise.

If you have some time to spare, you can easily create simple support materials that will make acting the story more fun. Why not encourage your child to help with these? (The same materials could be used for Sunday school or classroom play.) Here are some ideas:

● In a darkened room, a lighted torch provides all that is needed for "Let there be light".

● Light the room as the plants grow. Children can hold leaves and branches—either real or cut from card—to indicate the earth full of plants.

- A yellow balloon makes a lovely sun, otherwise colored card sun, moon and star shapes can be waved aloft—hung from strings attached to bamboo sticks.
- Cut out and color exotic birds to fly in the sky—any shape will do to fly about on a string.
- Cut out and color fish shapes and attach these to lengths of cotton or string. These can be towed across the ground to represent the living things in the sea.
- If animal toys are not available, freely imagined animal shapes can be cut from card and moved about by the children.

All those acting can dance about, waving sun, moon, stars, and birds and animals. Everyone can give a cheer to God for the wonderful things he has made for our world.

Story text and illustrations copyright © 1995 Leon Baxter
This edition copyright © 1995 Lion Publishing
Additional material by Christine Cousins

The author asserts the moral right
to be identified as the author of this work

Published by
Lion Publishing
20 Lincoln Avenue, Elgin, IL 60120, USA
ISBN 0 7459 3190 1

First edition 1995
10 9 8 7 6 5 4 3 2 1 0

Library of Congress CIP Data applied for

Printed and bound in Singapore